FIGHTER PLANES

BY

BILL GUNSTON OBE FRAeS

The First Fighters

*I*n 1903 the Wright brothers made the first successful airplane flights in the United States. Seven years later, the British Secretary of State for War said, *"We do not consider that airplanes will be of any possible use for war purposes."* This view was held by officials around the world, including in France, which rapidly became the center of aviation pioneering. However, in 1912 the British military formed the Royal Flying Corps (RFC) to fly reconnaissance missions to see what enemy troops were doing. Just for fun, the pilots began firing at kites with rifles and revolvers. By 1913 one of the first military aircraft was put on display by the Vickers company. Called the "Experimental Fighting Biplane," it was specially designed so that a machine gun could be mounted in the nose. When war broke out in Europe in August 1914, Vickers was contracted to produce 50 of their FB.5s and by 1915 over 100 had been sent to France with the RFC squadrons, primarily instructed to ram any Zeppelins encountered on their way. Without parachutes, this was not an exciting prospect for the untrained pilots, who resourcefully wore car tires in case they came down in the English Channel. Before long, two-seater planes were carrying observers with rifles and revolvers trained on the enemy, and combat aircraft became a reality. All this must have been a great shock to those who had written off airplanes as useless in wartime.

ZEPPELIN AIRSHIPS

Before the First World War began in 1914 the idea of airplanes in war was remote, but the use of airships was a possibility. Both the German Army and Navy used airships, and from 1915 they used them to drop bombs on Britain. It took airplanes to shoot them down.

WRIGHT BROS. BIPLANE.

WRIGHT BIPLANE

In August 1910 Lt. Jake Fickel, of the U.S. Army, flew as a passenger in a Wright biplane and fired four shots from a Springfield rifle at a target almost 3 feet (1 meter) square on the ground. He scored two hits. He was the first man ever to fire a gun from an airplane.

EXPÉRIENCES DE LANCEMENT DE BOMBES EN AÉROPLANE

THE FRENCH AIR CORPS

This illustration depicts early maneuvers by the French Air Corps in 1913, showing them dropping bombs from airplanes.

VICKERS GUNBUS

In February 1913, what could be called the first British military aircraft was put on display by Vickers at an Aero Show in London. This "Experimental Fighting Biplane" (EFB) had quite a short central body (a "nacelle") with the engine at the back driving a pusher propeller. This meant that the tail had to be attached by four thin rods (called booms), which were far enough apart to leave room for the propeller. This rather strange arrangement was adopted so that the company's own Vickers-Maxim machine gun could be mounted in the nose, fed by a long belt of ammunition. It was aimed by a gunner in the front cockpit. Just behind him was the pilot. This "pusher" arrangement was later used by many types of aircraft, including the FB.5 (Fighting Biplane, type 5), popularly called the Gunbus, which was active in the First World War.

THE PILOT'S SIDEARM

After the War began most reconnaissance pilots carried a personal "sidearm," for possible use to avoid capture after being shot down. This Webley pistol was a favorite for British pilots.

GUNBUS COCKPIT

Pilots soon discovered that they needed instruments to help them fly. The first were a tachometer (showing how fast the engine was turning), an altimeter (showing how high the airplane was flying), and an airspeed indicator (showing speed through the air).

Dawn of Air Warfare

DROPPING BOMBS

The first bombers were often ordinary aircraft fitted with a bomb-dropping mechanism invented and fitted on the spot. An even simpler answer was for the crew to hang the bombs beside the cockpits and drop them by hand.

In 1912 the British government decided that perhaps airplanes might have some military use. They organized a competition, entered by Geoffrey de Havilland with his B.E.1. Although he did not win, he continued to improve his straight biplane, which became the Royal Flying Corps' most numerous type in the First World War. It was a B.E. that was to claim the first air combat victory on August 25, 1914, only three weeks after the start of the War. Three B.E.2s chased a German aircraft for miles before the German pilot, realizing he could not get away, landed in a field. Both occupants escaped to a nearby wood. The British pilots ran after them, brandishing pistols, but returned to set fire to the enemy aircraft and then took off again. A month later, Frenchman Sergeant Joseph Frantz suddenly came up behind a German Aviatik. His Voisin plane was armed with a Hotchkiss machine gun. Quickly his observer, Corporal Louis Quénault, aimed at the enemy aircraft and shot it down. This was the first aircraft actually shot down in air warfare, and the dawn of the airplane as a weapon of war.

MACHINE GUN

It was the machine gun that transformed airplanes into fighters. In the First World War almost all the machine guns fitted to aircraft were originally designed for use by soldiers on the ground. Many French aircraft used this type of Hotchkiss machine gun, mounted on pivots and aimed by the observer. He was usually in a cockpit behind the pilot, but in the Voisin he was in front.

THE "BLÉRIOT EXPERIMENTAL" OR B.E.2

Louis Blériot was a Frenchman who made monoplanes, but his name became synonymous with the RFC for airplanes with a propeller on the nose. De Havilland's B.E.2 was popular with the RFC. It was very stable in flight, which meant it could fly without the pilot touching the controls. Therefore both pilot and observer could watch the battlefield below and write down anything of interest. This stability made the aircraft difficult to maneuver, which was disastrous against the new German planes in the First World War.

NATIONAL MARKINGS c.1915

Once the War began it was soon realized that aircraft had to be painted with a clear indication of their nationality, so ground soldiers did not shoot at their own aircraft. Soon simple national markings were devised.

Great Britain   *Russia*   *Belgium*   *Italy*   *Germany*

MONOPLANE FIGHTERS

The British thought monoplanes were unsafe, but the French Morane-Saulnier firm made them in large numbers. This Type L monoplane had the wing passing through the fuselage (body), while other Moranes had it fixed above the fuselage on struts.

The Fokker Scourge

FOKKER EINDECKER

In 1915-16 these highly maneuverable little monoplanes struck fear into the hearts of Allied aviators. They so dominated the skies over the Western Front that the British aircraft, such as the B.E.2s, were called "Fokker fodder." Later in 1916 they faded from the scene, because aircraft were becoming stronger and more powerful.

Even before the start of the First World War several farsighted people had come to the conclusion that the best way for an airplane to shoot down an enemy would be for it to have a machine gun fixed to fire straight ahead. It would be aimed by maneuvering the whole aircraft. Thus, the pilot need be the only person on board, and the aircraft could be smaller and more agile than a two-seater. Of course, with the propeller at the front there was a problem. The French pilot, Roland Garros, just fixed strong steel deflectors to the propeller of his Morane L monoplane at the beginning of the War and quickly destroyed four German aircraft. When Garros was himself shot down, the Germans discovered his idea, and asked Anthony Fokker to copy it. Fokker came up with something better – he invented a way to synchronize the gun to the speed of the propeller, so it only fired when there was no propeller blade in front. The result was the Fokker Eindecker. Though it was a low-powered little aircraft, its combination of adequate speed, excellent maneuverability, and a forward-firing machine gun made it deadly.

GERMANY'S TOP ACES

Here Baron von Richthofen, Germany's top ace, is surrounded by four of his pilots. When flying, they often left their caps behind but kept on their cavalry boots and heavy leather greatcoats in order to try to keep warm. Their counterparts in the RFC wore a strange double-breasted tunic (popularly called a "maternity jacket"), and increasingly wore specially designed calf-length soft boots lined with thick fur.

FOKKER TRIPLANE

Officially called the Dr.I, the brightly painted triplanes were as feared as the Eindecker had been previously. Allied planes were usually camouflaged, or just painted a dull olive-brown, but the best German fighters were organized into large groups called circuses, in which each pilot could choose to paint his aircraft in an individual scheme of vivid colors to frighten the enemy. This scarlet one is a replica of that used by the greatest of them all, Baron Manfred von Richthofen (the Red Baron). He held Germany's top-score of 80 victories when he was shot down and killed in April 1918.

ANTHONY FOKKER

Anthony Fokker was a Dutchman, but before the First World War he set up his aircraft factory near Berlin. By the end of the War he was famous (Americans would say infamous), and he had no difficulty in moving his factory to his native Amsterdam, where he made everything from fighters to airliners.

D.H.2

Captain Geoffrey de Havilland was one of the most famous British aircraft designers. In 1915 he designed the D.H.2, with a single cockpit in the nose fitted with a machine gun. The D.H.2 was a useful single-seater, but it was the later D.H.4, with its 375-horsepower engine, that became the Allies' most important anti-Zeppelin aircraft.

NIEUPORT XI

The French Nieuport company made some of the best single-seat fighters of their day. The Nie. XI was called *Le Bébé* because it was so small. It had only an 80-horsepower engine and weighed little more than 1,000 lb (454 kg). They were outstandingly agile biplanes that could easily catch the Fokkers and beat them in close combat.

Killing Machines

By 1916 air warfare was an accomplished fact. As well as the task of reconnaissance, aircraft had been developed to drop bombs, aim torpedoes at ships, and, not least, shoot down other aircraft. Combat aircraft were at first called "fighting scouts," but they gradually became known as "fighters" (except in the United States where, until the Second World War, they were called "pursuits"). The key to success in air combat was higher flight performance: faster speed, more rapid climb to greater altitudes, and ever-better ability to maneuver. These demands could only be met by fitting more powerful engines. Armaments were also important and many were developed during the First World War. Dozens of different small bombs were tried, and showers of darts. A few pilots even tried to snare enemy aircraft with grappling hooks at the end of a long cable! Night fighters also made their first appearance because of a need to find some aerial defense against German Zeppelin airships. Armed with a crew, machine guns, an electric generator, and a searchlight, they were too slow to be effective. Ordinary fighters were better, and in 1919 the best was the Fokker D.VII. Not particularly special, but extraordinarily effective, the Allies demanded the hand-over of every D.VII after the War.

TAKING AIM

On this British fighter, the S.E.5a (S.E. meant "scout experimental"), there are two types of gunsight – a ring-and-bead sight on the left used for close range, and an Aldis sight on the right, which contained lenses to see longer distances. There was a Vickers machine gun installed inside the nose, and on a special mounting above the upper wing was a drum-fed Lewis machine gun (above).

Compass

r.p.m. gauge (showing engine speed)

Cocking levers for the two Vickers guns

Ignition switches

Air speed indicator

Altimeter

Air pressure

Top of plane's control column

CAMEL COCKPIT

Most successful of all British fighters was the Sopwith Camel. It was said that looking ahead from a Camel cockpit was the most exciting view in the world, partly because the pilot looked over his two Vickers machine guns. By this time fighter cockpits had more instruments. The ignition switches, however, were clumsy circular units with brass covers exactly like those fitted to 1916 houses.

DOGFIGHT

By 1917 it was common for dozens of aircraft to engage in what became called "a dogfight." Each pilot tried to get on the tail of an enemy in order to shoot him down, while at the same time preventing any other enemy from getting on his own tail. Thus, he needed eyes in the back of his head. Here a Spad of RFC No. 23 Squadron tries to get on the tail of a Fokker D.VII marked with the simpler black cross that Germany introduced in 1918.

SPAD XIII

In 1915 French aircraft designer Louis Bechereau decided to use a completely new engine made by the Hispano-Suiza company (the name means "Spanish-Swiss" and is better known as a car manufacturer). It had eight water-cooled cylinders in two rows and gave 150 horsepower. The result was an excellent fighter called Spad VII, and 5,600 were made. Next came the Spad XIII, with the engine uprated to 220 horsepower, armed with two Vickers guns. No fewer than 8,472 were made by 1918.

BRISTOL FIGHTER

Officially called the Bristol F.2B, this was unusual in that it was a successful fighter with a crew of two. In both World Wars, the way to shoot down an enemy was to get "on his tail" and get the hostile aircraft in one's gunsight. While the Bristol pilot did this, the observer in the rear cockpit had either one or two Lewis machine guns that he could aim anywhere to the rear.

LEWIS MACHINE GUN

This gun was ideal for use by observers (backseaters), because it worked well even on its side or upside down, and was fed by a drum on top (holding either 47 or 97 rounds). Drums could be changed in seconds, the empty drum often being thrown overboard. The barrel was inside a fat casing containing cooling fins.

DEWOITINE D.520

In 1939 the French Dewoitine
company began making the D.520,
generally considered the best French
fighter of the Second World War.
Its 910-horsepower engine was
made by Hispano-Suiza, and it
was specially arranged so that a
big 20mm cannon could fit on top
of the crankcase firing through the
hub of the propeller. The D.520 also
had two machine guns in each wing,
and had a top speed of
329 mph (530 km/h).

BOEING F4B-1

The F4B family were U.S. Navy counterparts of
the Hawker Fury. They had another kind of engine in which
the cylinders were arranged radially like the spokes of a wheel
and covered in thin fins so that they could be cooled by air. The resulting aircraft looked much less streamlined;
but in fact the air-cooled radial was usually lighter. Since it was also shorter, it made the fighter more maneuverab
and it did not need a heavy drag-producing water radiator.

THE CHANGING ENGINE

In the First World War many fighters had rotary
engines such as the 130-horsepower Clerget (left).
The entire engine rotated together with the
propeller, and this acted like a top (a gyroscope)
and made piloting difficult. After 1918 designers
made static radials, such as the 450-horsepower
Bristol Jupiter (right). Apart from having nine
instead of seven cylinders, this differed in using
ordinary gasoline without lubricating oil having to
be added.

Between the World Wars

The First World War ended on November 11, 1918. For the next ten years there was little pressure to build better fighters, though engines developed dramatically. This development was further spurred by air racing. In 1931 a Rolls-Royce engine for racing developed 2,780 horsepower, though only for minutes at a time and using special fuels. Compared to the 130-horsepower engines on some fighters in the First World War, this was a huge leap and triggered the development of much better fuels for air force squadrons. Also, by 1930, a few designers were finding out how to make aircraft with a metal skin. The wire-braced biplanes of the past had fabric covering and these were replaced by all-metal "stressed-skin" monoplanes. This so dramatically reduced drag that fighter speeds jumped from 200 mph (322 km/h) to over 350 mph (563 km/h). In turn, this led to cockpits covered by transparent canopies, improved engine installations, flaps on the wings to slow the landing, and landing gears that could retract in flight. Some of these developments were opposed by fighter pilots, who could not believe that a fighter could be a sleek monoplane with an enclosed cockpit.

POLIKARPOV I-153

This Soviet biplane was unusual among biplanes in that it had retractable landing gear. The wheels folded directly backwards, at the same time rotating 90 degrees so that they could lie flat in the underside of the aircraft. The I-153 had a radial engine, but it was enclosed in a neat cowling to reduce drag. Thus, this fighter could reach 267 mph (430 km/h), about 62 mph (100 km/h) faster than the Fury and F4B.

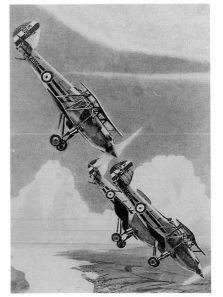

HAWKER FURIES

In the days before jet aircraft there were two basic kinds of engine. Some had their cylinders (usually 12) cooled by water and arranged in two lines. When installed in the aircraft they resulted in a long and pointed nose, as in these Fury fighters of the Royal Air Force (RAF) in 1932. This looked very streamlined, but in fact such engines needed a big radiator to cool the water and this slowed the aircraft down.

FAMOUS FIGHTERS

Whereas the Allies in the Second World War used dozens of different fighters, the German Luftwaffe relied on 33,000 Bf 109s, later joined by 20,000 Fw 190s. The Messerschmitt Bf 109 (in the distance) was first flown in April 1935, but by fitting more powerful engines and heavier armament it was kept formidable to the end of the War. Some Bf 109 pilots managed to shoot down over 300 enemy aircraft. The Spitfire (in the foreground) was the most successful Allied fighter and also the most famous. A later and more advanced design than the Hurricane, the Spitfire was developed through 24 versions, starting in 1938 weighing 5,500 lb. and with a speed of 362 mph, and ending in 1945 weighing 11,615 lb. and with a speed almost 100 mph greater!

HAWKER HURRICANE

Compared with the Bf 109, the British Hurricane was more primitive in design, being larger and, until 1941, covered in fabric like a fighter of the First World War. Major advantages of the Hurricane were that it was easy to fly, very tough, and easy to repair. In the Battle of Britain, Hurricanes shot down more German aircraft than everything else combined.

AFTER THE BATTLE

By the end of the War, towns and villages throughout Europe bore the scars of air attack. This town in Normandy (northern France) was actually fought over in 1944. Just outside would have been the RAF fighters, based on a hurriedly constructed airfield with the pilots living in tents. The runway would be a bulldozed field with a long strip of steel mesh laid down to give a smooth surface.

LEADERS OF THE LUFTWAFFE

In 1933 the German air force, forbidden after 1918, was reborn as The Luftwaffe. The Commander was Field Marshal Hermann Goering, who was to become a significant Nazi leader over the War period, and he appointed Ernst Udet (right) to choose the planes. Both men were fighter aces in the First World War.

The Second World War
The War in Europe

The Second World War (1939–45) firmly established the military role of airplanes. The Battle of Britain, which in the summer and autumn of 1940 certainly changed the entire course of history, was the first time since 1918 that large numbers of fighters had engaged in deadly air combat. This time, virtually all the fighters were streamlined stressed-skin monoplanes, with engines of over 1,000 horsepower and maximum speeds significantly higher than 300 mph (480 km/h). The combined Allied air forces in Britain were outnumbered by the German Luftwaffe (air force), and also had the disadvantage that Britain's airfields had been heavily bombed. However, the British had one huge advantage – the invention of radar. Instead of fighters flying aimlessly waiting for an enemy encounter, every Luftwaffe attack was plotted and pilots were given accurate directions for interception.

SPITFIRE PILOTS

The Second World War began in September 1939, and by the end of 1940 the RAF had lost more pilots than it had at the start. It was thus extremely important that hundreds of pilots found their way to England from the countries overrun by Germany, such as Poland, Czechoslovakia, France, Belgium, the Netherlands, Denmark, and Norway. Many others came from Commonwealth countries such as Canada, Australia, South Africa, and New Zealand. Without them, Britain's situation would have been even more serious.

The Second World War
The War in the Pacific

On December 7, 1941 the Japanese Imperial Navy Air Force attacked the U.S. Pacific Fleet at Pearl Harbor, in Hawaii. This act brought both countries into the War. At that time almost nothing was known about Japanese aircraft, the Allies having the idea that they were all flimsy inferior copies of American and British designs. Nothing could have been further from the truth! One fighter alone, the Navy Mitsubishi A6M2, commonly known as the Zero, shot down with ease every Allied aircraft it encountered. This was surprising since it had an engine of only just over 1,000 horsepower. After this shock, Japanese aircraft were taken very seriously. By 1944 many Japanese were flying Kamikaze suicide missions, deliberately crashing their bomb-laden aircraft onto Allied ships. Fighters found it difficult to defend against such attacks. Toward the end of the War, the Japanese best was the Nakajima Ki-84 Hayate (Gale). Gradually, such aircraft as the U.S. Navy F6F and F4U gained the upper hand.

KAMIKAZE PILOTS

In the final year of the War thousands of Japanese chose to undertake many kinds of suicide missions. These pilots had volunteered for Kamikaze missions. The Kamikaze was a great wind that, hundreds of years earlier, had scattered an enemy fleet. In October 1944 Japanese pilots first decided to load up their aircraft with explosives and crash them on enemy ships in the Philippines, and later at Okinawa. By 1944 the Imperial Navy even had tiny rocket aircraft, so fast they were almost impossible to shoot down, with the whole nose filled with explosives.

ADVERSARIES
IN THE SKY

Apart from the Imperial Army's Kawasaki Ki-61, all the mass-produced Japanese fighters had air-cooled radial engines. By 1943 these engines had been developed to over 1,900 horsepower, and this made possible even more formidable fighters. By this time such U.S. Navy fighters as the F6F Hellcat (right, taking off from an aircraft carrier) and F4U Corsair had achieved supremacy over the "Zero" and other 1,000-horsepower types, but the Imperial Army's Nakajima Ki-84 (left) was typical of the new species. Though it did not quite reach 400 mph (644 km/h), the Ki-84 was a brilliant all-around aircraft. However, most of the Japanese pilots were inexperienced, and they never again got the upper hand.

A JAPANESE ZERO

The Zero only had just over 1,000 horsepower, but it was so light it could outfly its opponents, and then destroy them with its two 20 mm cannon.

ENOLA GAY

great secrecy the United States, assisted by British scientists, had invented atomic bombs, one of which could destroy a city. On August 6, this B-29, named "Enola Gay" after the aircraft commander's wife, dropped such a bomb on Hiroshima. Three days later another, named "Bock's Car," dropped a different kind of bomb on Nagasaki. The Japanese surrendered.

RECOGNITION BOOK

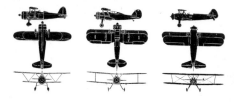

To the inexperienced eye, all aircraft (with some exceptions) look quite similar. Recognition manuals became standard issue for fighter pilots although many never became skilled at telling friend from foe. This page from a 1941 recognition book shows (from the left): a Fiat C.R.42, an Italian fighter; a Gloster Gladiator, a British fighter; and a Boeing (Stearman) PT-13, an American trainer.

THE SECOND WORLD WAR

This pilot (right) is wearing standard British flying clothing. The one-piece overall was pulled on from below and fastened with zips. In the front of the legs are pockets for maps and other documents (though pilots had to be very careful what they took with them over enemy territory). Most operational clothing could be plugged in and electrically heated. He is actually wearing his oxygen mask, so with goggles in place no part of his face is visible. His kit is completed by long cape-leather gloves and sheepskin-lined boots, and his seat-type parachute is on the ground.

PARATROOPS

This Italian magazine from about 1940 is making propaganda out of Italy's parachute troops, which used to descend from the sky to capture enemy targets. Such a means of attack was pioneered in the Soviet Union, and then adopted on a large scale by the Germans. Thousands of paratroops were used in Belgium in 1940 and to capture Crete in 1941. Even larger numbers were used by the British and Americans in 1944-45.

BETWEEN THE WARS

In the 1920s it gradually became universal for fighter pilots to wear parachutes. This Belgian pilot is wearing a British Irvin type of pilot parachute, with the canopy and shroud lines all tightly folded inside a pack that formed a cushion on which the pilot sat. The fighter's seat was an aluminium "bucket" type with a big hollow in which the parachute fitted. He wears a leather helmet, goggles (because he had an open cockpit), and cavalry type boots.

Fighter Pilots of the Past

MUSTANG PILOT

In the Second World War one of the best Allied fighters was the North American P-51 Mustang. This pilot would have much in common with pilots of the past, but much more equipment. His helmet would be fitted with headphones, and on the front it carried an oxygen mask (note the big pipe going to it) and integral microphone.

It seems astonishing today that the fighter pilots of the First World War did not have parachutes and were not even strapped into their cockpits. One of the greatest British aces, Major Albert Ball VC, was found one day lying dead on the ground. There was no aircraft near, and no German claimed to have shot him down, and it was thought he must have simply fallen out of his fighter. By the mid-1930s the fighter pilot climbed into his cockpit, sat on his parachute, strapped tightly into his seat, and then had to plug in both his radio cable and oxygen pipe. Training programs were also developed. Pilots would learn on simple primary trainers, and after as little as 40 hours, they would progress to more powerful trainers, such as the T-6 Texan (or Harvard). At something over 150 hours they would progress to operational fighters and would practice firing at targets towed on a long cable by special tug aircraft. By 1942 pilots were learning to drop bombs and fire rockets, both challenging tasks since the weapons had no built-in guidance as they do today.

WASPS

In the United States there were so many women pilots that many of them were organized into the Women's Auxiliary Service Pilots to ferry all kinds of aircraft from factory to squadron, and often to repair or modification centers.

BRISTOL BEAUFIGHTER

The Beaufighter was a massive, powerful, and tough long-range fighter with devastating armament of four cannons and six machine guns. Once it was equipped with radar it proved ideal as a night fighter, entering RAF service in this role in late 1940.

Night Fighters

A few aircraft in World War I were intended for fighting at night, especially against airships, but the technology for such a task did not exist. By World War II it was commonplace for aircraft to fly at night, but it was still almost impossible to hunt down enemy aircraft on a dark night. The breakthrough was the development of radar sets small enough to be carried inside aircraft. Such AI (Airborne Interception) radar is comprised of boxes of electronics and various antennas. These aim an electronic beam into the sky ahead, while other antennas pick up reflections from enemy aircraft. Primitive AI in 1940 was bulky and heavy, and needed skilled operators. Thus, the AI-equipped fighter had to be large and powerful. The first successful type was the Bristol Beaufighter, used in the War to shoot down Luftwaffe bombers, and later to fire torpedoes and rockets against enemy ships. In 1942 came the de Havilland Mosquito. Faster than the "Beau," this brilliant aircraft served as a bomber, a day and night fighter and attack aircraft, a long-range reconnaissance aircraft, and even for goods transport. Soon the Luftwaffe was fitting radars into their aircraft, and from 1943 they also added a new kind of armament installation, in the form of powerful cannon firing at a steep angle upwards. This meant they could attack from underneath and Allied planes literally never knew what hit them.

MOSQUITO COCKPIT

The de Havilland Mosquito was even better than the Beaufighter. Although it was made of wood, it was one of the fastest aircraft in the sky, and it could fly almost any kind of mission. The pilot sat on the left in a rather "cosy" cockpit, with the navigator on his right, just far enough back for elbows not to clash. Here the pilot's controls of a Mk XII night fighter are on the left, beyond the top of his control column, with its gun-firing button. On the right are the radar displays and controls, managed by the navigator.

LUFTWAFFE NIGHT FIGHTER

First flown in May 1936, the Messerschmitt Bf 110 was planned as a formidable twin-engined, long-range fighter to escort the Luftwaffe bombers. In the Battle of Britain they proved easy targets for Hurricanes and Spitfires, but were about to become very useful. Fitted with more powerful DB 605 engines, and with a crew of three, they were packed with radar in order to find RAF bombers at night. This late-1944 Bf 110G-4B/U1 has a mass of radar antennas on the nose, as well as special exhausts that showed no visible flames at night.

THE BEST NIGHT FIGHTER PILOT

Major Heinz Wolfgang Schnaufer shot down an amazing 121 RAF heavy bombers at night. He survived the War, only to be killed soon afterward in a traffic accident.

SCHRÄGE MUSIK

This is German for "slanting music," or jazz. It was their code name for a special kind of armament for night fighters. Two or more heavy cannons would be installed in the middle of the fighter, pointing steeply upwards at 70 to 80 degrees. Skilled pilots would find an RAF heavy bomber and, positioning themselves underneath it, would aim the guns at the spars of the wing. A quick burst and the bomber would lose a wing. Provided the fighter got out of the way of the falling bomber there was no danger, because the RAF bombers were totally "blind" underneath.

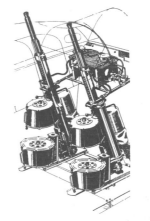

BLACK WIDOW

In the United States, Northrop created one of the first aircraft ever planned as a night fighter from the outset. This big machine had a bulging central nacelle packed with radar, guns, and a crew of three. The tail was carried on two booms. Fully loaded, the P-61 Black Widow weighed up to 15 tons.

The First Jets

Towards the end of the Second World War, the engines of the latest war planes were cumbersome masses of metal weighing over a ton, but with every part made like a fine Swiss watch. Even though the latest fighters had become heavier, the massive engines could propel them at over 450 mph (724 km/h). But it was almost impossible to make traditional fighters go any faster. Even more serious was the fact that ordinary propellers were reaching a fundamental speed limit. Thus the fighters of 1944-45 were the end of an era. In both Britain and Germany the turbojet engine was being developed. Frank Whittle had invented the first turbojet engine in Britain in 1929 but nobody was interested. Six years later, in Germany, Hans von Ohain thought of the same idea. The first jet aircraft flew in Germany in August 1939. Nothing much happened to Whittle's engine until one was sent to the USA. Then things moved fast, and the first Allied jet fighter, the American Bell P-59 Airacomet, flew on October 2, 1942. However, the much greater German effort resulted in a multitude of jet aircraft. The most important was the Messerschmitt Me 262, and, had the Germans not been defeated in 1945, their jets would have been a big problem for the Allies.

A NEW BREED OF PILOT

R.P. "Bee" Beamont was a fighter pilot throughout the War, and afterwards he became even more famous in Britain as a test pilot. He tested Hawker Typhoons and Tempests, followed by Gloster Meteor jets and many other types, before becoming Chief Test Pilot on the Canberra jet bomber, Lightning, TSR.2, Jaguar, and Tornado.

ROCKET INTERCEPTOR

The Messerschmitt Me 163B was a strange tailless rocket interceptor with the pilot in the nose along with two 30-mm cannons. Behind him were tons of deadly liquids that fed a rocket engine in the tail. It was a tricky "last-ditch" weapon that killed many of its own pilots.

FE 500

GLOSTER METEOR

First of the British jets, the Gloster Meteor
had two Whittle-type engines, and first
flew in March 1943. This was one of the
prototypes, as indicated by the big
"P" in a circle. After the War, a later
version set a speed record at over
616 mph (975 km/h).

MESSERSCHMITT
Me 262A-1A

The Me 262 was a superb
all-around fighter and fighter-
bomber powered by two Jumo 004B turbojets
slung under the wings. In the nose was the formidable
armament of four 30-mm cannons. With a speed of 525
mph (845 km/h), it was much faster than any Allied aircraft.
The Me 262 would have been even more of a problem to
the Allies had not Adolf Hitler misguidedly decreed that
they all be used as bombers.

LAVOCHKIN La-7

At the end of the Second World War the Russians
had no jet aircraft, and typical of their fighters
was the La-7, powered by a 2,000-
horsepower piston engine. For the
desperately harsh conditions on
the Russian front aircraft had
to be very tough and simple.
The La-7 was nevertheless
at least equal to fighters
from any other country.

SIR FRANK WHITTLE

As a young and very junior RAF pilot in 1929, Frank
Whittle invented the turbojet. He proved mathematically
that it could work, but his superiors in the Air Ministry
were not interested. At his own expense, he took out
a patent, finally granted in January 1930, but still
nobody showed the slightest interest. At last, in
desperation, he and a group of friends found just
enough money to actually build a turbojet, which
he started up on April 12, 1937. This amazed the
officials and experts, but by this time hundreds
of engineers were working on jets in Germany,
and theirs was the first jet aircraft to fly.

GIANT AIRCRAFT CARRIERS

After the Second World War the U.S. Navy began building aircraft carriers much bigger than any previous warships. Today 13 are in service, each with a displacement of up to 102,000 tons. The flight deck is over 1,000-ft. (300-meters) long, and there are over 40 mess decks (restaurants) for the 6,000 ship's crew and aircrew on board. Each evening those off duty have a choice of 25 movies. When in action, the rapid launch and recovery of aircraft is almost like a ballet, with differently colored deck crews each playing a choreographed role.

LANDING ON A CARRIER

This Boeing F-18 Hornet is about to hit the deck of a U.S. Navy carrier. The pilot has lowered the landing gear and the long arrester hook at the tail, and put the wing in the high-lift configuration with the leading and trailing edges all hinged sharply downwards. Guided by electronic systems (in the old days pilots were guided by a batsman standing on deck with things like brightly colored table-tennis bats) the pilot aims to hit the deck just beyond the first of several arrester wires stretched across the ship. The long hook should pick up one of these strong cables even before the wheels brutally slam onto the deck. The momentum of the aircraft pulls the wire out, resisted by a system of cable drums, stopping the aircraft sharply.

THE SEA VIXEN

This big de Havilland aircraft had powerful radar in the nose operated by a second crew member in what was called "the coal hole" low down on the right of the pilot. The armament was a mixture of four large guided missiles and various rockets or bombs. Vixens could dive faster than sound.

Naval Jets

From the earliest days of fighters, attempts had been made to operate them from warships. Naval planes had been launched from lighters (flat barges) towed behind fast destroyers. In the Second World War fighters operated from British, American, and Japanese aircraft carriers. Most did not last long, because they tended to crash on returning to the ship. But by the end of the War, in August 1945, aircraft designers knew how to make naval aircraft strong enough to stand up to the violent stresses of being shot off catapults, smashed down on heaving decks, and then suddenly brought to a halt by arrester wires. There was also a need to have folding wings, so that they could be taken down in small elevators and tightly packed in hangars. By the time peace returned, jet fighters were taking over, with improved electronic navigation aids. In the 1950s a series of new ideas were introduced: the angled flight deck, the powerful steam catapult, and the mirror sight to help guide pilots on deck in bad weather.

UNFOLDING THE WINGS

This Grumman F9F of the U.S. Navy's "Blue Angels" aerobatic team is unfolding its wings before being catapulted off the deck of an aircraft carrier. Naval aircraft are designed to fold their wings so that more can be packed into congested hangars below deck. The F9F entered service soon after the Second World War, and saw service in the Korean War of 1950-53.

SIDEWINDER MISSILE

The Sidewinder was invented by the U.S. Navy in 1953 as a guided missile able to home (steer itself) onto the heat radiated by a target aircraft. Originally weighing only just over 100 lb. (45 kg), it was the simplest and cheapest guided missile in its class. The heat-seeking guidance was in the nose, steering the missile via the four pivoted nose fins. Next came the warheads, followed by the rocket motor. On the fixed tail fins were small flywheels that spun at high speed to give the weapon stability. They are named after a venomous snake, which, in the same way, senses heat emitted by its victims.

Supersonic Fighters

LIGHTNING

The prototype of this outstanding British fighter first flew on April 4, 1957. On the same day the Government said fighters were obsolete and that the RAF did not need any! This crippled the development of the Lightning, and the RAF and British aircraft industry took years to recover. Uniquely, the Lightning had a wing swept back at 60 degrees and two Rolls-Royce Avon turbojets, one above the other. The bulge underneath is an extra fuel tank, and the small projections on each side of the nose carried missiles (not fitted here). The Lightning could reach twice the speed of sound.

In 1945 documents captured from Germany showed that jets could be made to fly faster if their wings were "swept" (angled back like an arrowhead). The first such fighter to fly (in 1948) was the North American F-86 Sabre. It was 100 mph (161 km/h) faster than "straight-wing" jets and, in a dive, it could fly faster than sound. Residents of Los Angeles began hearing strange bangs, and it was soon realized that they were caused by the supersonic fighter's shockwaves reaching the ground. Designers began to fit more powerful engines so that fighters could fly faster than sound when level. The Convair F-102, a radar-equipped interceptor with a delta (triangular) wing and fin, was supposed to be supersonic but proved too slow. In 1954 it was urgently redesigned according to new aerodynamic discoveries and it reached Mach 1.25 (1.25 times the speed of sound) with the original engine. By 1956 it was developed into the F-106, exceeding Mach 2 and setting a record at 1,525 mph (2,454 km/h). Many countries added to the sophistication of design, engine power, and aerodynamics of the supersonic fighter, but no other aircraft has yet matched the Soviet MiG-31 and MiG-31M for their combined speed and range, their power, radar ability, and enormous air-to-air missiles.

A DOUBLE DELTA

The Swedes called their Saab 35 Draken (Dragon) a double delta because it had a delta wing mounted on the ends of an inner wing of an even more extreme delta shape. Thus, all the fuel tanks, electronics, and other items were arranged from front to rear. Despite its amazing shape, the Draken prototype, flown in 1955, was very successful, and eventually Saab built 600, including a few for Denmark and Finland. Some were passed on from Sweden to the Austrian air force. Drakens had the same engine as the Lightning, but half as many of them.

DELTA-WING FIGHTER

The F-102A had wings and a vertical tail that were in a perfectly triangular shape (named "delta" after the Greek letter). This shape enables the wing to be very thin yet stronger than wings of ordinary shape; and the short span (distance from tip to tip) makes it suitable for supersonic speeds. The penalty of small wings is the need for longer runways as such aircraft need to take off and land at high speeds.

"MISSILE WITH A MAN IN IT"

This is what Lockheed called their F-104 Starfighter when it was revealed in 1956. It was designed to meet the criticisms of U.S. pilots who had fought in the Korean War and had been outflown by the MiG-15. It was designed to climb very steeply and fly faster than any enemy plane. Features included a single powerful engine, tiny razor-edged wings, a high tailplane, and a pilot seat that ejected downwards.

"CHUCK" YEAGER

Major (later General) Charles E. Yeager was a fighter pilot in the United States Army Air Force (USAAF) during the Second World War. In peacetime he became a test pilot and flew the Bell XS-1 to become the first human to fly faster than the speed of sound on October 14, 1947.

Today's Pilots

The enormous increase in military flying in World War II led to rapid technical advances of all kinds, though many did not come into use until the conflict was over. Several of these developments affected pilots' clothing. In a steep turn, with the wings banked to an angle of 60 degrees, the acceleration is 2g (twice gravity), so your weight appears to have doubled. Planes at the end of the World War II could reach about 6g, so the pilot had to keep a tight hold of the stick (control column) to stop his arm from being wrenched off downwards. A sustained 6g turn will make most people "black out"; they remain conscious but their eyes go dark and they can no longer see. Vision is restored on recovery to straight and level flight. To help counter this and other problems of violent maneuvers, a special kind of flying clothing was developed.

COMBAT SIMULATOR

Whereas flight simulators help pilots to learn to master their aircraft, a combat simulator trains them to dogfight with enemy aircraft. It is inside a giant dome, on the inside of which the pilot sees the ground, the sky, and other aircraft. Today there are so many computer games that there are thousands of potential fighter pilots!

MODERN PILOT

Comfortable in a Mk 14 ejection seat, this fighter pilot is all geared up, ready for action. Modern fighter seats are very complex and sat much more than a complex Second World War fighter.

FIGHTER COCKPIT

This is the cockpit of an F-16 Fighting Falcon simulator. In the distance, "enemies" can be seen. The pilot gets all the information he needs from the large square displays in front of him, each like a clever reprogrammable TV. Some guide his flight and help him find enemies, while others tell him about his own aircraft. Whereas other fighters have a traditional big control column ("joystick"), the F-16 pilot flies holding a small grip shaped to fit his hand on the right edge of the cockpit.

BONEDOME HELMET

Today, fighter pilots wear a strong but light helmet that protects their heads if they should be violently bumped against the cockpit canopy. In combat, pilots were sometimes knocked out when

26

LIMB GARTERS

Both the pilot's legs are encircled by strong straps, one above the knee and the other around the calf. On ejection, the legs are pulled in and the pilot's arms are also restrained to avoid hitting the cockpit or being injured by windblast.

BOOTS

Fighter pilots wear strong boots with long laces. These help him push hard on the rudder or wheel brake pedals and protect him if he has to eject.

"TOP GUN"

This Hollywood blockbuster starring Tom Cruise as a maverick U.S. fighter pilot also stars two of today's top fighter planes – the Grumman F-14 Tomcat carrier-based fighter of the U.S. Navy, and the Soviet MiG.

FIRING HANDLE

Between the pilot's thighs is the black and yellow striped firing handle. This triggers a complicated computer-controlled sequence on which his life depends.

THE FLYING SUIT

Even today the standard attire of a fighter pilot is the overall. This Japanese pilot is not ready to fly. His cap would be replaced by the complex "bonedome" helmet with oxygen mask, communications, and other services

EJECTION!

After the Second World War it was found that jet aircraft could fly so fast that, in an emergency, the pilot could not just "bale out." To escape by parachute he had to be shot out. Gradually ejection seats were made safer (early types sometimes painfully damaged the spine) and today the Martin-Baker Mk 14 is typical of the refined types on offer. Modern seats are shot out by a propulsion system incorporating a rocket, which can be seen firing here. A small chute is deployed to slow the seat down. Finally, the pilot is released from the seat as his own parachute deploys automatically.

Today's Fighters

*I*t is remarkable that the history of the fighter plane has seen just 30 years of piston-engined fighters (1915-45) and over 50 years of jets. In this time, fighters have become bigger and heavier, far more powerful, incredibly more complicated, and much more expensive. An unexpected development in today's fighters is that instead of the fighter getting faster, it has almost gone in reverse. In 1954 the first supersonic fighters reached over Mach 1 and went on to reach Mach 2. The MiG-25 nudged Mach 3. At such a speed aircraft must travel in almost straight lines. To maneuver, that speed must be brought right down. The French Dassault Mirage family all reached Mach 2.2, but their latest fighter, the Rafale, cannot exceed Mach 1.8. Some of the greatest of today's fighters are products of the former Soviet design teams, such as MiG and Sukhoi. Both have twin engines hung under a very efficient wing, which, merged into the body and with powerful horizontal tails and twin fins, gives it outstanding maneuverability.

THE GREATEST?

One of the largest modern fighters is the Sukhoi Su-27, designed in Moscow and produced by a factory in Komsomolsk-na-Amur in far Siberia. It could be clumsy and unimpressive, but, in fact, many experts consider it the most formidable in the sky. Powered by two AL-31 engines, it has tremendous performance, and such test pilots as Evgenii Frolov have demonstrated maneuvers – such as the upward-tilt "Cobra" – that no Western fighter can copy. Su-27s and various successors carry a spectrum of missiles far superior to anything currently available in the West.

A COBRA MANEUVER

This maneuver was first performed in 1989 by Sukhoi test pilot Viktor Pugachev. He astonished the world by rotating his aircraft, nose up, through 120 degrees and then back to horizontal, with the flight path remaining horizontal.

PRODUCTION LINE

In 1972 the United States Air Force (USAF) invited manufacturers to submit ideas for a "light fighter," much cheaper than the massive F-15 Eagle then in production. There was no suggestion the winner would actually be put into production, much less adopted by the USAF; but before long the General Dynamics F-16 Fighting Falcon had gained so many customers it had far surpassed the F-15. Today a product of Lockheed Martin, later versions of F-16 are still in production at this factory in Fort Worth, Texas.

COST OF MODERN FIGHTERS

In the Second World War a Spitfire cost about $9,900, but today a single F-22 (left) costs over $99,000,000. Thus, for the price of one modern fighter, one could in theory have bought 10,000 Spitfires.

FIGHTER ENGINE

Today all fighters have turbofan engines, in which the air coming in at the inlet is divided. Some air is compressed and then goes through the combustion chamber and turbines, while the rest is bypassed and mixed with the hot gas at the back. This Russian AL-31FP is one of a pair fitted to the Su-27 (see page 28). It has a maximum thrust of 29,320 lb. (13,300 kg), and a special feature is that its jet nozzle can be vectored (swivelled) to exert powerful control on the aircraft. On top are all the fuel controls, starter, electric generator, hydraulic pumps, and other accessories.

SEA HARRIER

In the Falklands War in 1982 the British Aerospace Harrier of the RAF and Sea Harrier of the Royal Navy enabled the Argentine invaders to be defeated. Without these quite small aircraft it would have been impossible even to consider retaking the islands. No other aircraft can rule the skies and also attack ground targets without needing an airfield. This is because of the development of jet nozzles, which can be directed downwards so the aircraft can take off and land vertically.

RAFALE

France's next-generation fighter is the Rafale (French for "squall"). Made by the Dassault Company, which since 1955 has delivered thousands of Mirage fighters, the Rafale has two engines and a controllable foreplane just above and ahead of the delta wing. Different versions are being produced for the Armée de l'Air (air force) and Aéronavale (navy). This Rafale has a clumsy fixed probe on the nose for taking on fuel in flight; most flight-refueling probes are retractable

A EUROFIGHTER COCKPIT

Best of the future European fighters is the Eurofighter, made by Britain, Germany, Italy, and Spain in collaboration. Here, beyond the advanced ejection seat, can be seen the control column and then the instrument panel dominated by big multifunction displays. These displays are blank as much as possible showing the pilot only what he needs to know. Should anything go wrong he can push buttons to find out as much detail as he wishes. In the center of the windshield is the optically flat glass of the computerized gunsight.

F-22 RAPTOR

This strange name, meaning a bird of prey, has been chosen for the most important fighter in production today, being produced by Lockheed Martin, for tomorrow's USAF. It is a very large aircraft; yet because it is specially designed for what is called "stealth," it will be almost invisible on enemy radars. It has a huge wing and large tailplanes, and all the missiles are carried internally. Beside the fuselage are the big lozenge (diamond) shaped air inlets.

Fighters for the Millennium

Until the jet era, new fighters could be designed, developed, and put into production in a few weeks. Today, despite computers that can slash the time needed for complex calculations, the same tasks can take up to ten years. Thus, the Eurofighter was a detailed feasibility study in 1984, but will not enter service until after 2002. Cooperation among Britain, Germany, Italy, and Spain was slow, but the Eurofighter eventually flew in March 1994. However, when test flying began, it had long been obvious that future fighters should have vectoring nozzles, able to swivel so the plane could thrust in different directions.

Such nozzles may be available at the Eurofighter's midlife update in 2007. Shape is also central to the performance of future fighters – to reduce the size of the reflection on enemy radar screens. The Lockheed Martin F-22 Raptor, the newest fighter in the world, has two very powerful engines whose nozzles cannot only vector but also discharge the jets through flat slits. This is all part of the trend towards "stealth" design, which makes the fighters hardly detectable on enemy radar. After the F-22, the next generation is the JSF (Joint Strike Fighter), a U.S. multiservice program in which Britain has a small share. Some designs have powerful engines with the VTOL (vertical takeoff and landing) capability of the Harrier.

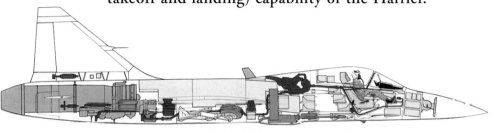

GRIPEN

Probably the smallest fighter in production in the world is Sweden's Saab Gripen (Griffin). It has an engine similar to that of the Hornet (see page 23), but only one instead of two. Like the Rafale, the Gripen has a foreplane, and a delta wing, a gun in the fuselage, and missiles under the wing and on the wingtips.

DID YOU KNOW?

In the Soviet Union bombers were fitted with fighters to protect them. Vladimir Vakhmistrov conducted experiments that in November 1935 culminated in a TB-3 heavy bomber taking off with an I-15 biplane fighter on top of each wing and an I-16 monoplane fighter under each wing. An I-Z monoplane fighter then approached and hooked on under the fuselage, to make five fighters joined to one bomber! If enemy aircraft appeared, they were all to unlatch and zoom off.

Arguments have raged over which was the first jet fighter. The first to fly was the German Heinkel He 280, which never went into production. The first to be delivered to a customer was the American Bell YP-59A Airacomet, delivered to the United States Army Air Force (USAAF) on September 30, 1943. The first delivered to a front-line regular squadron was the British Gloster Meteor, to 616 Squadron on July 12, 1944. And yet most experts think it should be the German Me 262. Suffice to say, in the Second World War, the Me 262 was the best jet fighter, and by far the most numerous.

The XF-85 Goblin unfolded its wings in flight. This tiny jet fighter had folding wings to fit inside one of the B-36 bomb bays. If enemy fighters appeared, the XF-85 was to be released. After dropping like a stone, its pilot would unfold the wings and do battle with the enemy. Afterwards he was to hook back on for the long ride home.

The fastest fighter in regular service was the Soviet Union's MiG-25. Powered by two huge R-15B-300 engines, it could fly long distances at 1,864 mph (3,000 km/h), or nearly three times the speed of sound.

In 1914, Pemberton-Billing designed, built, and test-flew a successful fighter in seven days. The corresponding time for the development of the Eurofighter is 20 years (1982-2002).

In both World Wars a typical effective life for a fighter was two months. Today the RAF Jaguars are to serve 40 years (1972-2012), while the German Bachem Ba349 of 1944 was designed to fly a single mission only.

ACKNOWLEDGMENTS

We would like to thank: Graham Rich, Del Holyland of Martin-Baker, Rosalind Beckman and Elizabeth Wiggans for their assistance.
First edition for the United States, Canada, and the Philippines published by Barron's Educational Series, Inc., 1999
First published in Great Britain in 1999 by *ticktock* Publishing Ltd., The Office, The Square, Hadlow, Kent, TN11 0DD, United Kingdom
Copyright © 1999 ticktock Publishing Ltd. American edition Copyright © 1999 Barron's Educational Series, Inc.
All rights reserved. No part of this publication may be reproduced in any form, by photostat, microfilm, xerography, or any other means, or incorporated into any information retrieval system, electronic or mechanical, without the written permission of the copyright owner.
All inquiries should be addressed to: Barron's Educational Series, Inc., 250 Wireless Boulevard, Hauppauge, New York 11788, http://www.barronseduc.com
Library of Congress Catalog Card No. 98-74956
International Standard Book Number 0-7641-0645-7
Picture research by Image Select. Printed in Hong Kong.
98765432

AKG Photo London: OFC (dog fight), 7b, 12br, 12bl, 15tl. Ann Ronan@Image Select: 2tl, 2bl. Aviation Photographs International: OFC (main pic: Francois Robineau, Dassault/Aviaplans), 3bl, 3br, 6tl, 7t, 8b, 9c, 11tr, 12tl, 15c, 18/19b, 20/21t, 21tr, 22tl, 22bl, 22/23c, 23tr, 24b, 25t & OFC, 26l, 28b, 30tl, 30/31c, 30cl. Bundesarchiv: 18/19c. Colorific: 31tr. FPG International: 14tl, 15b, 26tl, 30bl. Hulton Deutch: 13tr, 13b, 14b, 17bl, 21br. Hulton Getty: 4tl. Image Select: 3tl & OFC, 20bl. Kobal Collection: 27tr & OBC. Kozlowski Productions: 17tr & IFC. Mary Evans Picture Library: 3tr, 5tr, 5cr, 7cl, 7cr, 8/9t, 10t, 11br, 16c. Martin-Baker: 16/17c, OFC. Philip Jarrett: 6/7, 8tl, 10bl, 10br, 10/11 & OFC, 15tr, 18tl, 18bl, 19tr, 20/21b, 24tr, 29tr, 27bl, 29b & OBC. Quadrant Picture Library: 5b, 9t, 16tl & OFC, 20tl, 28tl, 26r. Salamander Picture Library: 4/5b & OBC, 9b, 12c, 16/17c & OBC & 32, 23bl, 24/25, 26bl, 31bl. Yefim Gordon: 29r,

Every effort has been made to trace the copyright holders and we apologize in advance for any unintentional omissions.
We would be pleased to insert the appropriate acknowledgment in any subsequent edition of this publication.

BARRON'S